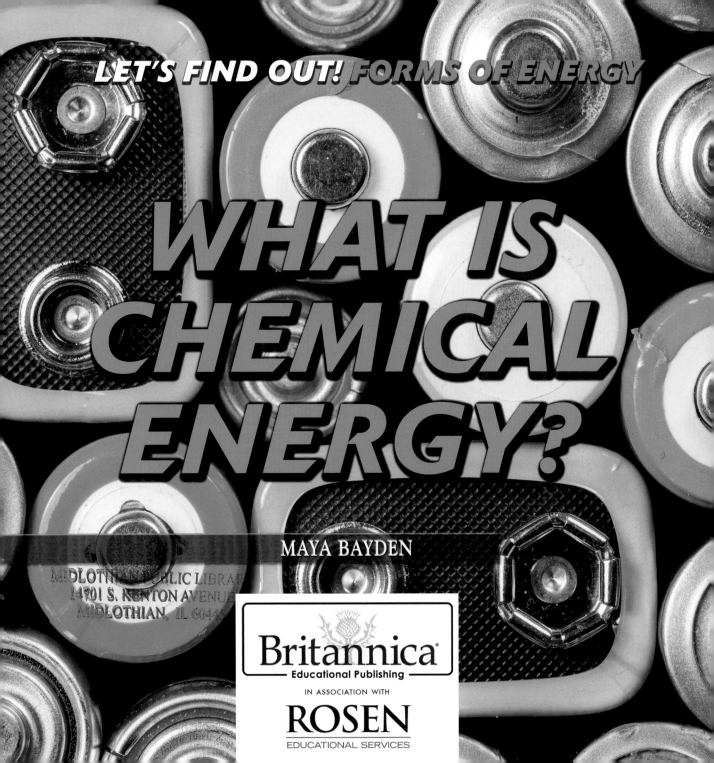

WHAT IS CHEMICAL ENERGY?

MAYA BAYDEN

Britannica
Educational Publishing

IN ASSOCIATION WITH

ROSEN
EDUCATIONAL SERVICES

Published in 2018 by Britannica Educational Publishing (a trademark of Encyclopædia Britannica, Inc.) in association with The Rosen Publishing Group, Inc.
29 East 21st Street, New York, NY 10010

Distributed exclusively by Rosen Publishing.
To see additional Britannica Educational Publishing titles, go to rosenpublishing.com.

First Edition

Britannica Educational Publishing
J.E. Luebering: Executive Director, Core Editorial
Mary Rose McCudden: Editor, Britannica Student Encyclopedia

Rosen Publishing
Amelie von Zumbusch: Editor
Nelson Sá: Art Director
Nicole Russo-Duca: Designer
Cindy Reiman: Photography Manager
Karen Huang: Photo Researcher

Library of Congress Cataloging-in-Publication Data

Names: Bayden, Maya.
Title: What is chemical energy? / Maya Bayden.
Description: First edition. | New York : Britannica Educational Publishing in association with Rosen Educational Services, 2018. | Series: Let's find out! Forms of energy | Audience: Grades 1-4. | Includes bibliographical references and index.
Identifiers: LCCN 2016058552 | ISBN 9781680486957 (library bound : alk. paper) | ISBN 9781680486933 (pbk. : alk. paper) | ISBN 9781680486940 (6-pack : alk. paper)
Subjects: LCSH: Energy conversion—Juvenile literature. | Chemical kinetics—Juvenile literature. | Fuel—Juvenile literature. | Energy transfer—Juvenile literature. | Power resources—Juvenile literature. | Plants—Photorespiration—Juvenile literature.
Classification: LCC TK2896 .B39 2018 | DDC 541/.39—dc23
LC record available at https://lccn.loc.gov/2016058552

Manufactured in the United States of America

Photo credits: Cover, p. 1 silabob/Shutterstock.com; p. 4 Gajus/Shutterstock.com; p. 5 JGI/Jamie Grill/Blend Images/Getty Images; p. 6 Tuomas Lehtinen/Shutterstock.com; p. 7 Christos Siatos/Shutterstock.com; pp. 8, 10, 21, 25, 26, 29 Encyclopædia Britannica, Inc.; p. 9 Courtesy of the United States Mint; p. 11 Zerkut/Shutterstock.com; p. 12 bondgrunge/Shutterstock.com; p. 13 mhatzapa/Shutterstock.com; p. 14 wavebreakmedia/Shutterstock.com; p. 15 © iStockphoto.com/Peeter Viisimaa; p. 16 ArtDi101/Shutterstock.com; p. 17 Pyty/Shutterstock.com; p. 18 Ammit Jack/Shutterstock.com; p. 19 Hero Images/Getty Images; p. 20 CNRI/Science Photo Library/Getty Images; p. 22 Stolyevych Yuliya/Shutterstock.com; p. 23 John Burke/Photolibrary/Getty Images; p. 24 Martin Leigh/Oxford Scientific/Getty Images; p. 27 Ed Aldridge/Shutterstock.com; p. 28 Italianvideophotoagency/Shutterstock.com; interior pages background image Yevhen Tarnavskyi/Shutterstock.com.

Contents

What Is Energy? 4

Chemical Elements 8

Chemical Reactions 10

Potential and Kinetic Energy 14

Photosynthesis 16

Cellular Respiration 18

Fermentation 22

Batteries 24

Fuel Cells 26

Internal-Combustion Engines 28

Glossary 30

For More Information 31

Index 32

What Is Energy?

Energy is another word for power. It is one of the most basic ideas in science. A simple definition of energy is the ability to do work. Energy makes things move. It makes plants and animals grow, and it makes machines work. All activity in the universe can be explained in terms of energy and matter.

Energy is important, but it can be a bit complicated to understand.

Plants absorb energy from the sun and then use that energy to grow.

The food that we eat gives us the chemical energy we need for our bodies to do work.

That is because energy exists in many different forms. Some of the forms of energy are heat, light, electrical energy, chemical energy, mechanical energy, and sound energy. We encounter these forms of energy in our life every day. For example, the food we eat contains chemical energy. Most cars, trucks, buses, and motorcycles run on the chemical energy that is stored in gasoline.

THINK ABOUT IT

How might other forms of energy be converted into heat energy?

One form of energy can change into another form of energy. In a lightbulb, for example, electric energy changes to light and heat. When you burn a piece of wood in a campfire or a fireplace, the chemical energy of the wood changes to heat and light. Our bodies get the energy they need to grow, move, and think from the chemical energy stored in the foods we eat. Batteries also contain stored chemical energy. When you use batteries in a flashlight, the chemical energy from the batteries is changed into electricity and then into light.

Batteries store chemical energy, which can change into electricity.

Burning wood converts chemical energy into heat energy and light energy.

The fact that one form of energy can convert, or change, into another makes it easier for people to get the energy they need. If people need light, they can convert the chemical energy in candles into light energy. Or they can convert the electricity running to a lamp into light.

CHEMICAL ELEMENTS

Chemical elements are the building blocks for all matter. They are basic substances that cannot be broken down into simpler substances. Every element has a symbol. The symbol for an element is sometimes the first letter of its name. H is the symbol for the element hydrogen and O is the symbol for oxygen.

The smallest unit of an element is called an atom. Atoms can be combined with other atoms to form

This image shows three different ways to represent a water molecule.

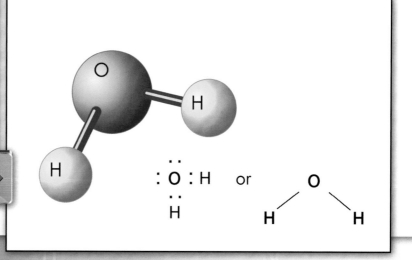

Gold is a very valuable chemical element. It is represented by the symbol Au.

molecules. For example, one oxygen atom and two hydrogen atoms combine to make a water molecule (H_2O).

COMPARE AND CONTRAST

How are atoms and molecules similar? How are they different?

Some substances are made up of molecules that contain just one type of chemical element. Oxygen gas (O_2) is made up of molecules of just oxygen atoms. Other substances are made up of molecules that contain atoms of two or more different chemical elements. Such substances are called chemical compounds. Water is a chemical compound because its molecules have two hydrogen atoms and one oxygen atom.

CHEMICAL REACTIONS

The atoms in molecules are held together by chemical energy. All atoms are made up of smaller particles called electrons, protons, and neutrons. Strong chemical bonds are formed whenever atoms share electrons. Electrons are found alone or in pairs in the outer part of atoms. When two atoms with unpaired electrons get close, their unpaired electrons may form a pair. Both atoms then share the pair. This holds the atoms together.

Chemical energy holds the particles of an atom together. This image shows two kinds of atoms.

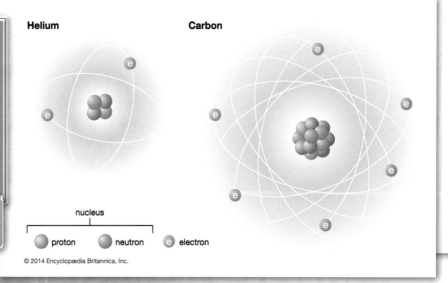

Helium

Carbon

nucleus

proton   neutron   e electron

© 2014 Encyclopædia Britannica, Inc.

◀◀

Rust is the result of a chemical reaction that occurs between iron and water.

When chemical bonds between atoms are formed or broken, chemical reactions occur. A chemical reaction is a process in which one or more substances are converted to one or more different substances. In a reaction, the atoms of the starting substances are rearranged, forming new substances with different properties. Energy plays a key role in chemical reactions. Breaking bonds requires energy, while forming bonds releases energy.

Dynamite gives off a lot of energy when it explodes. It is used to break up Earth's surface to make mines.

When chemicals are mixed together to make dynamite, an explosion can occur if the person mixing the chemicals isn't careful. An explosion is a chemical reaction that gives off a tremendous amount of energy. Many reactions give off energy without being explosive. In these types of reactions, the energy required to break bonds is less than the energy released as new bonds form. Heat energy is often released from these types of reactions.

When an egg is fried, a chemical reaction occurs in which heat is absorbed by the molecules of the egg.

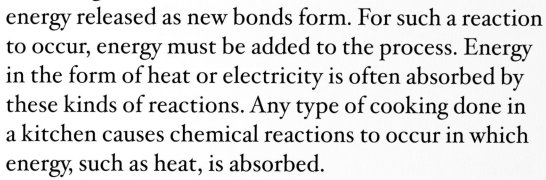

In other types of chemical reactions, the energy required to break bonds is greater than the energy released as new bonds form. For such a reaction to occur, energy must be added to the process. Energy in the form of heat or electricity is often absorbed by these kinds of reactions. Any type of cooking done in a kitchen causes chemical reactions to occur in which energy, such as heat, is absorbed.

COMPARE AND CONTRAST

How are a burning candle and a frying egg similar? How are they different?

POTENTIAL AND KINETIC ENERGY

All forms of energy can be described as either potential energy or kinetic energy. Potential energy is stored energy that comes from an object's position or state. Chemical energy is a form of potential energy that is stored in the bonds of molecules. For example, potential energy is stored in a stretched-out rubber band or in the bonds of molecules that make up the gasoline inside a car's gas tank. If the person stretching the rubber band lets go, the rubber band will snap. If a driver starts a car engine, the gasoline is burned, which is a

An arrow drawn back in a bow has a lot of potential energy.

The gasoline in a car's tank is a type of potential energy in the form of chemical energy.

chemical reaction that releases a lot of energy—enough to drive the engine.

As the rubber band and the car move, they gain kinetic energy. Kinetic energy is the energy of moving things. An object's potential energy has the ability, or potential, to turn into kinetic energy.

THINK ABOUT IT

What is another everyday example of chemical energy changing into kinetic energy?

PHOTOSYNTHESIS

During photosynthesis, plants convert light energy from the sun into food.

One of the most important forms of chemical energy is food energy. Photosynthesis is the name of the process that plants, algae, and certain other organisms use to transform light energy from the sun into the chemical energy of food. Photosynthesis is very important to life on Earth, because almost all living things depend on plants for food.

Photosynthesis starts when a green substance in plants, called chlorophyll, absorbs energy from sunlight.

The body of this giraffe uses the chemical energy stored in the leaves that it eats.

THINK ABOUT IT

Animals that only eat other animals are called carnivores. How do you think carnivores get chemical energy?

Plants also take in water from the ground and carbon dioxide from the air. They use the light energy to change water and carbon dioxide into oxygen and sugars. The plants use some of the sugars and store the rest. The oxygen is released into the air. Animals that eat plants use the chemical energy stored in the sugars to get the energy they need to stay alive.

Cellular Respiration

Cellular respiration is the process by which organisms use oxygen to break down food molecules to get chemical energy. This chemical energy provides the energy that cells need to function. Cellular respiration takes place in the cells of all living things, including animals, plants, fungi, and algae.

Cellular respiration occurs in this dog's cells.

18

Oxygen found in the air we breathe is necessary for cellular respiration.

Cellular respiration is a chemical reaction. During cellular respiration, a sugar called glucose is broken down in the presence of oxygen. This process releases chemical energy and produces carbon dioxide and water as waste products. This is represented by the chemical equation glucose + oxygen → chemical energy + carbon dioxide + water. Glucose and oxygen (on the left of the arrow) are the reactants of the reaction. Chemical energy, carbon dioxide, and water (on the right side of the arrow) are the products of the reaction.

Most cellular respiration takes place in specialized parts of the cell, called mitochondria. Mitochondria's main job is to produce chemical energy through cellular respiration. Some cells, such as those in the liver or muscles, have lots of mitochondria.

The chemical energy released in cellular respiration is captured in molecules called adenosine triphosphate, or ATP. ATP molecules leave the mitochondria and supply chemical energy to other places in the cell where it is needed. Cellular respiration also releases hydrogen and carbon. The hydrogen combines with oxygen to produce water and the carbon combines with oxygen to produce carbon dioxide. The water and carbon dioxide that are

The blue organelles in this image are the mitochondria in a fat cell. Mitochondria produce chemical energy.

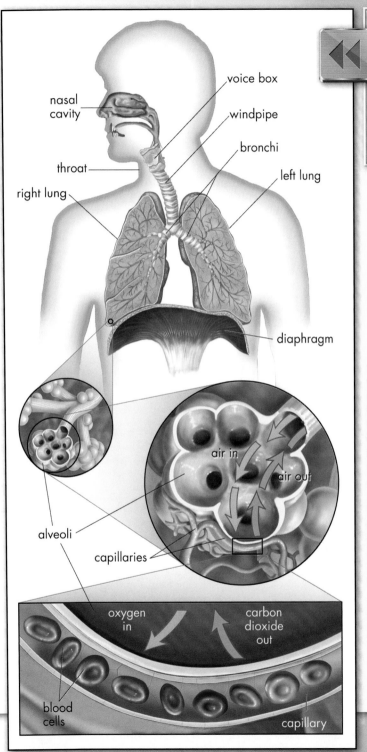

right lung
nasal cavity
throat
voice box
windpipe
bronchi
left lung
diaphragm
alveoli
capillaries
air in
air out
oxygen in
carbon dioxide out
blood cells
capillary

This diagram shows how our lungs exchange oxygen for carbon dioxide.

formed during cellular respiration are released from the cell as waste products into the bloodstream.

THINK ABOUT IT

ATP molecules are chemical compounds. Once ATP reaches the parts of a cell that need energy, what do you think happens to the compound so that its energy is released?

FERMENTATION

For cellular respiration to happen, oxygen must be present. But without oxygen, cells can still get chemical energy in a different way. This process is known as fermentation. Fermentation is a chemical change that happens in vegetable and animal substances. Fermentation often happens through the work of tiny living things called yeasts, bacteria, and mold. These living things create substances called enzymes. The enzymes break down food, such as glucose, into chemicals.

For thousands of years people have used fermentation to make bread, wine, beer,

Fermentation causes bread to rise. Yeast breaks down sugars, releasing carbon dioxide gas.

Cheese comes from milk or cream that has been fermented by bacteria.

cheese, and other foods. When bakers add yeast to bread dough, the yeast breaks down the sugars in the dough. While this happens, carbon dioxide gas is released, making the bread rise. People eat many other fermented foods. Cheese and soy sauce are also made by fermentation. In addition, scientists use fermentation to make certain drugs and vitamins.

COMPARE AND CONTRAST

How are cellular respiration and fermentation similar? In what important ways are they different?

BATTERIES

Batteries give electric power to flashlights, radios, cell phones, handheld games, and other types of equipment. Batteries store chemical energy and convert it into electrical energy when they are used.

Inside a battery there are two pieces of metal in a liquid or a paste. These metal parts are called electrodes. The liquid or paste, called an electrolyte, is a mix of chemicals. Each electrode has a point, called a terminal, that sticks out of the battery.

For a battery to work, the terminals must be linked by an outside wire. Then the chemicals in the electrolyte cause electrons to flow from one electrode to the other. A flow of electrons is an electric current. The electric current

This flashlight converts chemical energy from batteries into light.

flowing through the wire is what makes flashlights and other electric equipment work. Eventually the electrolytes get used up, and the battery no longer makes electricity.

THINK ABOUT IT

Some batteries can be recharged with an electric current from another source. How might this work?

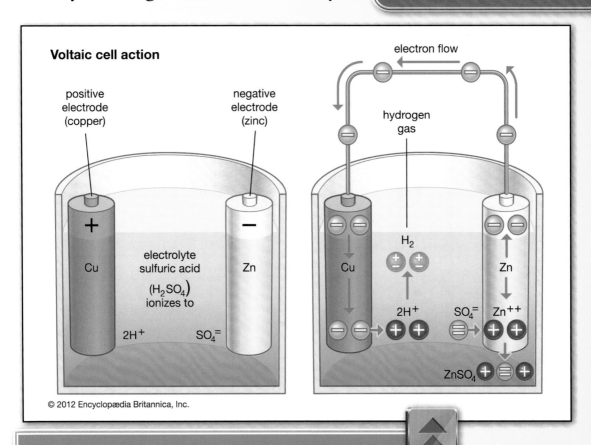

Voltaic cell action

electron flow

positive electrode (copper)

negative electrode (zinc)

hydrogen gas

+

−

Cu

electrolyte sulfuric acid

(H_2SO_4) ionizes to

Zn

$2H^+$

$SO_4^=$

H_2

Cu

Zn

$2H^+$

$SO_4^=$

Zn^{++}

$ZnSO_4$

© 2012 Encyclopædia Britannica, Inc.

For batteries to form a current, their electrodes must be connected by a wire.

FUEL CELLS

Fuel cells are another device that convert chemical energy into electrical energy. Fuel cells can supply electricity for a much longer period than batteries. They are used to provide power in large buildings such as hospitals.

A fuel cell is actually made up of a group of cells. Each of the cells is similar to a battery in that it has two electrodes and an electrolyte, which make an electric current. However fuel cells work

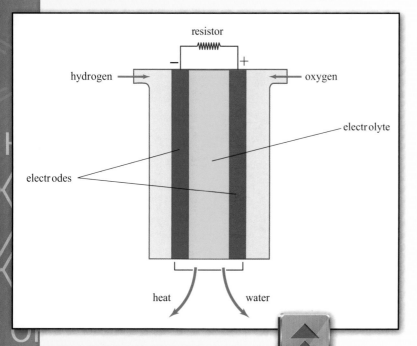

resistor

hydrogen → ← oxygen

electrolyte

electrodes

heat   water

The hydrogen and oxygen supplied to a fuel cell produce electricity.

Fuel cells are used to provide energy to some kinds of vehicles, such as this car.

differently than batteries by combining oxygen and fuel to produce electricity. Fuels such as hydrogen gas, methanol, or natural gas are broken down into hydrogen ions and electrons. Adding oxygen causes the electrons to move through an outside circuit.

COMPARE AND CONTRAST

How are fuel cells and batteries similar? How are they different?

The stored chemical energy in batteries eventually is used up. However, fuel cells never change. They continue to work because of a constant outside supply of fuel and oxygen.

Internal-Combustion Engines

Engines powered by internal **combustion** run cars, airplanes, and other machines. Internal-combustion engines burn fuel, like gasoline, to do work. This process converts chemical energy into mechanical energy.

In the engine, moving parts called pistons slide up and down in cylinders. Valves at the top of the cylinders let in fuel and air and let out burned fuel. Spark plugs ignite the fuel.

As the engine runs, it goes through a cycle of movements.

Motor boats are powered by internal-combustion engines.

Vocabulary

Combustion is a chemical process in which substances combine with oxygen and burn fuel.

First valves open to fill the cylinders with fresh fuel and air. Next, the pistons squeeze, or compress, the fuel and air into a small space, creating pressure. At this point, the spark plug ignites the fuel. The explosion of the burning fuel moves the pistons down and up. The valves open as the pistons rise and push the exhaust gases produced by the explosion out of the cylinder. The moving pistons turn other parts of the engine to run the machine.

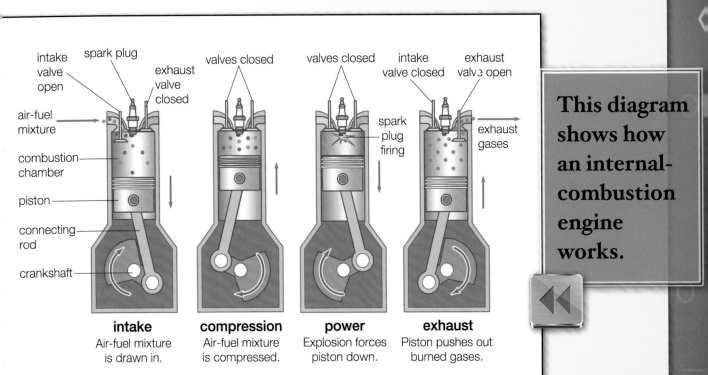

intake valve open
spark plug
exhaust valve closed
valves closed
valves closed
intake valve closed
exhaust valve open

air-fuel mixture
combustion chamber
piston
connecting rod
crankshaft

spark plug firing
exhaust gases

intake
Air-fuel mixture is drawn in.

compression
Air-fuel mixture is compressed.

power
Explosion forces piston down.

exhaust
Piston pushes out burned gases.

This diagram shows how an internal-combustion engine works.

GLOSSARY

algae A group of living things that resemble plants (but are not plants), belong to a group called protists, and make their own food by photosynthesis.

carbon dioxide A gas that is produced when people and animals breathe out or when certain fuels are burned and that is used by plants for energy.

chemical A substance that is formed when two or more other substances act upon one another or that is used to produce a change in another substance.

convert To change from one substance, form, use, or unit to another.

dynamite A blasting explosive that is mostly made up of nitroglycerin absorbed in another substance.

electrical energy The energy produced when charged particles flow from place to place.

electron An elementary particle that has a negative charge of electricity and travels around the nucleus of an atom.

fungi A group of living things (including molds, mildews, and mushrooms) that are neither plants nor animals and that feed on other life forms, most often on dead plants and animals.

glucose A sugar that is a source of energy for living things.

ignite To set on fire.

ion An atom that carries a positive or negative electric charge as a result of having lost or gained one or more electrons.

mechanical energy The total amount of energy an entire object has because of its motion and its position.

molecule The smallest unit of a substance that has all the properties of that substance.

organism An individual living thing.

oxygen A gas found in air that is necessary for life.

piston A sliding piece moved by or moving against the pressure of a fluid (as steam or hot gases) that usually consists of a short solid cylinder moving within a larger hollow cylinder.

reactant A substance that enters into and is changed by a chemical reaction.

FOR MORE INFORMATION

Books

Berne, Emma Carlson. *Transforming! Chemical Energy* (Energy Everywhere). New York, NY: PowerKids Press, 2013.

Johanson, Paula. *What Is Energy?* (Let's Find Out! Physical Science). New York, NY: Britannica Educational Publishing, 2015.

Wilson, Roman. *How Does a Battery Work?* (Electrified!). New York, NY: Gareth Stevens Publishing, 2013.

Winterberg, Jenna. *Chemical Reactions* (Physical Science). Huntington Beach, CA: Teacher Created Materials, 2016.

Zuchora-Walske, Christine. *Photosynthesis* (Science of Life). Minneapolis, MN: ABDO Publishing Company, 2014.

Websites

Because of the changing nature of internet links, Rosen Publishing has developed an online list of websites related to the subject of this book. This site is updated regularly. Please use this link to access the list:

http://www.rosenlinks.com/LFO/chemical

INDEX

adenosine triphosphate (ATP), 20, 21
atom, 8, 9, 10, 11

batteries, 6, 24–25, 26, 27

carbon, 20
carbon dioxide, 17, 19, 20, 23
cells, 18, 20, 21, 22
cellular respiration, 18–21, 22, 23
chemical compounds, 9, 21
chemical equation, 19
chemical reactions, 10–13, 15, 19
chlorophyll, 16
cylinders, 28, 29

electric current, 24–25, 26
electrodes, 24, 26
electrolyte, 24, 25, 26
electrons, 10, 24, 27
elements, 8–9
energy
    converting, 6–7

definition, 4
    forms of, 5
enzymes, 22
explosion, 12, 29

fermentation, 22–23
fuel cells, 26–27

gasoline, 5, 14, 28
glucose, 19, 22

heat energy, 6, 12, 13
hydrogen, 8, 9, 20
hydrogen gas, 27

internal combustion, 28–29

kinetic energy, 14, 15

light energy, 5, 6, 7, 16, 17

matter, 4, 8, 11
methanol, 27
mitochondria, 20
mold, 22

molecules, 9, 10, 14, 18, 20, 21

natural gas, 27
neutrons, 10

oxygen, 8, 9, 17, 18, 19, 20, 22, 27, 28

photosynthesis, 16–17
pistons, 28, 29
potential energy, 14–15
products, 19, 21
properties, 11
protons, 10

reactants, 19

terminals, 24

valves, 28, 29

water, 9, 17, 19, 20

yeast, 22, 23